Adult
MAD LIBS™

World's Greatest Word Game

He Loves Me, He Loves Me Not

By Roger Price and Leonard Stern

PSS!
PRICE STERN SLOAN

PRICE STERN SLOAN
Published by the Penguin Group
Penguin Group (USA) Inc., 375 Hudson Street, New York, New York 10014, USA
Penguin Group (Canada), 90 Eglinton Avenue East, Suite 700,
Toronto, Ontario M4P 2Y3, Canada
(a division of Pearson Penguin Canada Inc.)
Penguin Books Ltd., 80 Strand, London WC2R 0RL, England
Penguin Group Ireland, 25 St. Stephen's Green, Dublin 2, Ireland
(a division of Penguin Books Ltd.)
Penguin Group (Australia), 250 Camberwell Road, Camberwell, Victoria 3124, Australia
(a division of Pearson Australia Group Pty. Ltd.)
Penguin Books India Pvt. Ltd., 11 Community Centre,
Panchsheel Park, New Delhi—110 017, India
Penguin Group (NZ), 67 Apollo Drive, Rosedale, North Shore 0632, New Zealand
(a division of Pearson New Zealand Ltd.)
Penguin Books (South Africa) (Pty.) Ltd., 24 Sturdee Avenue,
Rosebank, Johannesburg 2196, South Africa

Penguin Books Ltd., Registered Offices:
80 Strand, London WC2R 0RL, England

Mad Libs format copyright © 2008 by Price Stern Sloan.

Published by Price Stern Sloan,
a division of Penguin Group (USA) Inc.,
345 Hudson Street, New York, New York 10014.

Printed in the United States of America. No part of this publication may be reproduced, stored
in any retrieval system, or transmitted, in any form or by any means, electronic, mechanical,
photocopying, or otherwise, without the prior written permission of the publisher.

ISBN 978-0-8431-3328-8

3 5 7 9 10 8 6 4 2

PSS! and MAD LIBS are registered trademarks of Penguin Group (USA) Inc.
Adult Mad Libs is a trademark of Penguin Group (USA) Inc.

Adult
MAD LIBS™

INSTRUCTIONS

MAD LIBS® is a game for people who don't like games!
It can be played by one, two, three, four, or forty.

• RIDICULOUSLY SIMPLE DIRECTIONS

In this tablet you will find stories containing blank spaces where words
are left out. One player, the READER, selects one of these stories. The
READER does not tell anyone what the story is about. Instead, he/she asks
the other players, the WRITERS, to give him/her words. These words are
used to fill in the blank spaces in the story.

• TO PLAY

The READER asks each WRITER in turn to call out words—an adjective or
a noun or whatever the space calls for—and uses them to fill in the blank
spaces in the story. The result is a MAD LIBS® game.

When the READER then reads the completed MAD LIBS® game to the other
players, they will discover that they have written a story that is fantastic,
screamingly funny, shocking, silly, crazy, or just plain dumb—depending
upon which words each WRITER called out.

• EXAMPLE (*Before* and *After*)

" _____ !" he said _____
          EXCLAMATION   ADVERB

as he jumped into his convertible _____ and
                                            NOUN

drove off with his _____ wife.
                          ADJECTIVE

" _____*Ouch*_____ !" he said _____*Stupidly*_____
          EXCLAMATION   ADVERB

as he jumped into his convertible _____*Cat*_____ and
                                            NOUN

drove off with his _____*brave*_____ wife.
                          ADJECTIVE

Adult
MAD LIBS™
QUICK REVIEW

In case you have forgotten what adjectives, adverbs, nouns, and verbs are, here is a quick review:

An **ADJECTIVE** describes something or somebody. *Lumpy, soft, ugly, messy,* and *short* are adjectives.

An **ADVERB** tells how something is done. It modifies a verb and usually ends in "ly." *Modestly, stupidly, greedily,* and *carefully* are adverbs.

A **NOUN** is the name of a person, place, or thing. *Sidewalk, umbrella, bridle, bathtub,* and *nose* are nouns.

A **VERB** is an action word. *Run, pitch, jump,* and *swim* are verbs. Put the verbs in past tense if the directions say PAST TENSE. *Ran, pitched, jumped,* and *swam* are verbs in the past tense.

When we ask for A PLACE, we mean any sort of place: a country or city *(Spain, Cleveland)* or a room *(bathroom, kitchen).*

An **EXCLAMATION** or SILLY WORD is any sort of funny sound, gasp, grunt, or outcry, like *Wow!, Ouch!, Whomp!, Ick!,* and *Gadzooks!*

When we ask for specific words, like a NUMBER, a COLOR, an ANIMAL, or a PART OF THE BODY, we mean a word that is one of those things, like *seven, blue, horse,* or *head*.

When we ask for a PLURAL, it means more than one. For example, *cat* pluralized is *cats.*

MAD LIBS® is fun to play with friends, but you can also play it by yourself! To begin with, DO NOT look at the story on the page below. Fill in the blanks on this page with the words called for. Then, using the words you have selected, fill in the blank spaces in the story.

Now you've created your own hilarious MAD LIBS® game!

HE LOVES ME,
HE LOVES ME NOT

PLURAL NOUN _____

NOUN _____

NOUN _____

NUMBER _____

ADJECTIVE _____

NOUN _____

NOUN _____

ADJECTIVE _____

A PLACE _____

ADJECTIVE _____

PART OF THE BODY _____

NOUN _____

PLURAL NOUN _____

You tell your friends you and your man are like two _____
PLURAL NOUN

in a pod. But does he feel the same way? To find out if he's your true

_____, select the scenario that best describes what
NOUN

happened following your last date:

(a) Your _____ didn't ring for _____days.
NOUN   NUMBER

(b) He sent you _____ flowers the next day, along
ADJECTIVE

with a handwritten _____ inviting you to the
NOUN

premiere of the latest Steven Spielberg _____.
NOUN

(c) You received an e-mail that said: I had a really _____
ADJECTIVE

time with you the other night at (the) _____.
A PLACE

(d) You never heard from the _____ guy again.
ADJECTIVE

If you answered (b) or (c), there's a chance you're truly the apple

of his _____. If you answered (a) or (d), don't put all
PART OF THE BODY

your eggs in one _____. It would be best to cut your
NOUN

_____ and keep looking.
PLURAL NOUN

FROM ADULT MAD LIBS™: HE LOVES ME, HE LOVES ME NOT. Copyright © 2008 by Price Stern Sloan,
a division of Penguin Group (USA), 345 Hudson Street, New York, NY 10014.

MAD LIBS® is fun to play with friends, but you can also play it by yourself! To begin with, DO NOT look at the story on the page below. Fill in the blanks on this page with the words called for. Then, using the words you have selected, fill in the blank spaces in the story.

Now you've created your own hilarious MAD LIBS® game!

LOVE POTION #9

NOUN _____

ADJECTIVE _____

ADJECTIVE _____

NUMBER _____

TYPE OF LIQUID _____

NOUN _____

NUMBER _____

ADJECTIVE _____

NOUN _____

ADVERB _____

ADJECTIVE _____

ADJECTIVE _____

NUMBER _____

ADJECTIVE _____

NOUN _____

NOUN _____

ADVERB _____

ADJECTIVE _____

Legend has it that if you make this potion and serve it to your

_____ , he will be your _____ love
    NOUN   ADJECTIVE

forever. This _____ recipe has been passed down
                    ADJECTIVE

through _____ generations. To make it yourself,
              NUMBER

combine two cups of _____ , one teaspoon of
                          TYPE OF LIQUID

granulated _____ , _____ ounces of
                  NOUN   NUMBER

_____ chocolate, and a dash of _____ .
      ADJECTIVE   NOUN

Then, _____ blend all of the ingredients together,
            ADVERB

stirring the _____ potion in a/an _____
                  ADJECTIVE   ADJECTIVE

direction for at least _____ minutes. Pour the
                              NUMBER

liquid into a/an _____ glass and top with a/an
                      ADJECTIVE

_____ . Serve to your significant _____ ,
      NOUN   NOUN

sit back, and watch it take effect. You'll _____ enjoy
                                                  ADVERB

the _____ results!
        ADJECTIVE

FROM ADULT MAD LIBS™: HE LOVES ME, HE LOVES ME NOT. Copyright © 2008 by Price Stern Sloan,
a division of Penguin Group (USA), 345 Hudson Street, New York, NY 10014.

MAD LIBS® is fun to play with friends, but you can also play it by yourself! To begin with, DO NOT look at the story on the page below. Fill in the blanks on this page with the words called for. Then, using the words you have selected, fill in the blank spaces in the story.

Now you've created your own hilarious MAD LIBS® game!

THREE LITTLE WORDS

NOUN _____

PLURAL NOUN _____

ADJECTIVE _____

ADJECTIVE _____

NOUN _____

ADJECTIVE _____

NOUN _____

TYPE OF LIQUID _____

ADJECTIVE _____

PART OF THE BODY _____

ADVERB _____

VERB ENDING IN "ING" _____

NOUN _____

Adult MAD LIBS™
THREE LITTLE WORDS

It's Valentine's Day, and you and your _____ have

NOUN

been dating for seven _____. Alas, he still hasn't

PLURAL NOUN

spoken those three _____ words you really want

ADJECTIVE

to hear. But you have a/an _____ feeling that

ADJECTIVE

tonight's the _____. First, he surprises you with a/an

NOUN

_____ dinner under the light of the _____.

ADJECTIVE   NOUN

Then he pops open a bottle of expensive _____ and

TYPE OF LIQUID

says he has something _____ to tell you. You lean in

ADJECTIVE

until your _____ is pressed up against him. "Yes?" you

PART OF THE BODY

ask _____. "I really enjoy _____ with

ADVERB   VERB ENDING IN "ING"

you," he says. "I'm so glad you're my best _____."

NOUN

FROM ADULT MAD LIBS™: HE LOVES ME, HE LOVES ME NOT. Copyright © 2008 by Price Stern Sloan,
a division of Penguin Group (USA), 345 Hudson Street, New York, NY 10014.

MAD LIBS® is fun to play with friends, but you can also play it by yourself! To begin with, DO NOT look at the story on the page below. Fill in the blanks on this page with the words called for. Then, using the words you have selected, fill in the blank spaces in the story.

Now you've created your own hilarious MAD LIBS® game!

THE BOY NEXT DOOR

ADJECTIVE _____

NOUN _____

ADVERB _____

PART OF THE BODY _____

ADJECTIVE _____

PART OF THE BODY (PLURAL) _____

NOUN _____

ADJECTIVE _____

ADJECTIVE _____

ADJECTIVE _____

ADVERB _____

ADVERB _____

NOUN _____

NOUN _____

NOUN _____

NOUN _____

ADJECTIVE _____

PART OF THE BODY (PLURAL) _____

ADJECTIVE _____

Adult MAD LIBS™
THE BOY NEXT DOOR

The selection of _____ guys in my apartment
                          ADJECTIVE

_____ is terrible. The one guy on my floor wears
        NOUN

_____ thick glasses and looks like he hasn't washed his
      ADVERB

_____ in weeks. But then one _____ day,
  PART OF THE BODY   ADJECTIVE

I got on the elevator and couldn't believe my _____.
                                          PART OF THE BODY (PLURAL)

I figured a new _____ must have moved in! He
                        NOUN

was incredibly _____ , with _____ hair and
                      ADJECTIVE   ADJECTIVE

_____ eyes. I was _____ amazed
      ADJECTIVE   ADVERB

when he started to flirt _____ with me and then
                                  ADVERB

asked me out! It was _____ at first sight. But when
                              NOUN

we both got off the _____ on the same floor, and
                            NOUN

he opened the door to my nerdy neighbor's _____ ,
                                                        NOUN

I was thrown for a/an _____ . It was the neighbor!
                              NOUN

He had a/an _____ makeover from his head to his
                    ADJECTIVE

_____ . And, believe it or not, now I'm dating this
  PART OF THE BODY (PLURAL)

_____ hunk!
      ADJECTIVE

FROM ADULT MAD LIBS™: HE LOVES ME, HE LOVES ME NOT. Copyright © 2008 by Price Stern Sloan,
a division of Penguin Group (USA), 345 Hudson Street, New York, NY 10014.

MAD LIBS® is fun to play with friends, but you can also play it by yourself! To begin with, DO NOT look at the story on the page below. Fill in the blanks on this page with the words called for. Then, using the words you have selected, fill in the blank spaces in the story.

Now you've created your own hilarious MAD LIBS® game!

GIFT IDEAS FOR HIM

ADJECTIVE _____

ADJECTIVE _____

NOUN _____

PLURAL NOUN _____

NOUN _____

ADJECTIVE _____

ADJECTIVE _____

NOUN _____

PART OF THE BODY (PLURAL) _____

ADJECTIVE _____

VERB _____

NOUN _____

ARTICLE OF CLOTHING _____

NOUN _____

Adult MAD LIBS™
GIFT IDEAS FOR HIM

It's not easy to find a/an _____ gift for your guy on
                               ADJECTIVE

Valentine's Day. If you're having trouble thinking of something, here

are some _____ ideas:
              ADJECTIVE

• Make a home-cooked _____ featuring his
                           NOUN

favorite _____. For dessert, bake a heart-shaped
              PLURAL NOUN

_____ with _____ frosting.
      NOUN   ADJECTIVE

• Write a/an _____ poem. Put it in a/an _____,
                  ADJECTIVE   NOUN

apply red lipstick to your _____, and seal it
                               PART OF THE BODY (PLURAL)

with a/an _____ kiss.
               ADJECTIVE

• Make it personal. If he loves to _____, get him a/an
                                        VERB

_____.
      NOUN

As a last resort, buy yourself the sexiest _____ you can
                                            ARTICLE OF CLOTHING

find and surprise him by opening the _____ wearing
                                          NOUN

only that!

FROM ADULT MAD LIBS™: HE LOVES ME, HE LOVES ME NOT. Copyright © 2008 by Price Stern Sloan,
a division of Penguin Group (USA), 345 Hudson Street, New York, NY 10014.

MAD LIBS® is fun to play with friends, but you can also play it by yourself! To begin with, DO NOT look at the story on the page below. Fill in the blanks on this page with the words called for. Then, using the words you have selected, fill in the blank spaces in the story.

Now you've created your own hilarious MAD LIBS® game!

WHAT A GIRL WANTS

ADJECTIVE _____

NOUN _____

PLURAL NOUN _____

PLURAL NOUN _____

PLURAL NOUN _____

ADJECTIVE _____

ADJECTIVE _____

NOUN _____

ADVERB _____

ADJECTIVE _____

PART OF THE BODY _____

TYPE OF LIQUID _____

PLURAL NOUN _____

NOUN _____

NOUN _____

Do you have a/an _____ fantasy about the perfect
                    ADJECTIVE

Valentine's Day? Drop some hints to your special _____
                                                    NOUN

to make your _____ come true! For example:
               PLURAL NOUN

- If you want him to send you a bouquet of _____,
                                              PLURAL NOUN

  mention that your best friend received a dozen red

  _____ from her _____ other.
   PLURAL NOUN   ADJECTIVE

- Tell him your _____ job has you working morning,
                   ADJECTIVE

  noon, and _____, and you're _____
               NOUN   ADVERB

  exhausted. He may surprise you with a/an _____
                                             ADJECTIVE

  weekend getaway!

- Moan about your sore _____ and plant a bottle of
                          PART OF THE BODY

  massage _____ by the bedside.
           TYPE OF LIQUID

If he's still not getting the hint, send yourself a bouquet of fragrant

_____ and make him think they're from another
 PLURAL NOUN

_____. He'll be so jealous, you'll receive a really great
 NOUN

_____!
 NOUN

FROM ADULT MAD LIBS™: HE LOVES ME, HE LOVES ME NOT. Copyright © 2008 by Price Stern Sloan,
a division of Penguin Group (USA), 345 Hudson Street, New York, NY 10014.

MAD LIBS® is fun to play with friends, but you can also play it by yourself! To begin with, DO NOT look at the story on the page below. Fill in the blanks on this page with the words called for. Then, using the words you have selected, fill in the blank spaces in the story.

Now you've created your own hilarious MAD LIBS® game!

WEEKEND GETAWAY

A PLACE _____

ADJECTIVE _____

NOUN _____

TYPE OF LIQUID _____

ADJECTIVE _____

PLURAL NOUN _____

VERB ENDING IN "ING" _____

ADVERB _____

PART OF THE BODY (PLURAL) _____

ADJECTIVE _____

ADJECTIVE _____

NOUN _____

ADJECTIVE _____

NOUN _____

Adult MAD LIBS™
WEEKEND GETAWAY

You and your sweetheart are off to (the) _____ for
A PLACE

a/an _____ weekend getaway. When you check in to
ADJECTIVE

your rustic bed-and-_____, you discover there's no
NOUN

hot _____ in the bathroom, and the bed is extremely
TYPE OF LIQUID

_____. No sooner do you turn out the _____,
ADJECTIVE   PLURAL NOUN

than the innkeeper's dog begins _____
VERB ENDING IN "ING"

_____ and doesn't stop all night. Neither of you can
ADVERB

sleep. In the morning, you're both so tired you can barely keep

your _____ open. Things go from bad to
PART OF THE BODY (PLURAL)

_____ as your honey has a/an _____
ADJECTIVE   ADJECTIVE

reaction to the breakfast and ends up at the nearest emergency

_____. But all's well that ends well. After all, if you
NOUN

can survive this _____ weekend, you can survive any
ADJECTIVE

_____ together!
NOUN

FROM ADULT MAD LIBS™: HE LOVES ME, HE LOVES ME NOT. Copyright © 2008 by Price Stern Sloan,
a division of Penguin Group (USA), 345 Hudson Street, New York, NY 10014.

MAD LIBS® is fun to play with friends, but you can also play it by yourself! To begin with, DO NOT look at the story on the page below. Fill in the blanks on this page with the words called for. Then, using the words you have selected, fill in the blank spaces in the story.

Now you've created your own hilarious MAD LIBS® game!

VALENTINE'S DAY SURVIVAL GUIDE

NOUN _____

ADJECTIVE _____

PLURAL NOUN _____

ADJECTIVE _____

ADJECTIVE _____

VERB ENDING IN "ING" _____

ADJECTIVE _____

PART OF THE BODY _____

ADJECTIVE _____

NOUN _____

ADJECTIVE _____

ADJECTIVE _____

PLURAL NOUN _____

NOUN _____

PLURAL NOUN _____

NUMBER _____

Adult MAD LIBS™
VALENTINE'S DAY
SURVIVAL GUIDE

If you find yourself without a date on Valentine's Day, don't panic!

It's not the end of the _____ . You can still have a/an
                              NOUN

_____ day. For instance, you can:
      ADJECTIVE

- Plan a/an _____ night out with your _____
                    PLURAL NOUN   ADJECTIVE

  girlfriends. Go see a/an _____ movie or head to your
                                  ADJECTIVE

  local _____ alley.
        VERB ENDING IN "ING"

- Treat yourself to a/an _____ day at the spa. Have a/an
                                ADJECTIVE

  deep _____ massage and a/an _____ facial
         PART OF THE BODY   ADJECTIVE

  and top it off with a mud _____ .
                                    NOUN

- Do something _____ for someone else. Cook a/an
                      ADJECTIVE

  _____ meal for another single friend, or bake a batch of
      ADJECTIVE

  chocolate _____ and drop them off for the firemen at
                  PLURAL NOUN

  the nearest _____ station.
                    NOUN

- Send yourself a bouquet of _____ . Don't be
                                     PLURAL NOUN

  embarrassed: Studies show that _____ percent of
                                          NUMBER

  women do this every Valentine's Day.

FROM ADULT MAD LIBS™: HE LOVES ME, HE LOVES ME NOT. Copyright © 2008 by Price Stern Sloan,
a division of Penguin Group (USA), 345 Hudson Street, New York, NY 10014.

MAD LIBS® is fun to play with friends, but you can also play it by yourself! To begin with, DO NOT look at the story on the page below. Fill in the blanks on this page with the words called for. Then, using the words you have selected, fill in the blank spaces in the story.

Now you've created your own hilarious MAD LIBS® game!

LOVE AT FIRST BITE

PART OF THE BODY _____

ADJECTIVE _____

VERB ENDING IN "ING" _____

ADJECTIVE _____

NOUN _____

NOUN _____

NUMBER _____

NOUN _____

TYPE OF LIQUID _____

ADJECTIVE _____

TYPE OF FOOD (PLURAL) _____

ADJECTIVE _____

ADJECTIVE _____

ADVERB _____

NOUN _____

Adult MAD LIBS™

LOVE AT FIRST BITE

They say the way to a man's heart is through his _____.
                                                    PART OF THE BODY

Try cooking this _____ meal full of aphrodisiacs, and
                        ADJECTIVE

you're sure to have him _____ for more!
                             VERB ENDING IN "ING"

- Start with _____ oysters on the half _____.
                   ADJECTIVE   NOUN

- Serve a/an _____ of your favorite champagne. A
                     NOUN

  glass or _____ will relax him and stimulate his
                  NUMBER

  _____.
        NOUN

- Cook lobster and serve with drawn _____. For a side
                                        TYPE OF LIQUID

  dish, try stalks of _____ asparagus.
                           ADJECTIVE

- For dessert, dip fresh _____ in a/an _____
                          TYPE OF FOOD (PLURAL)   ADJECTIVE

  chocolate sauce.

- Finish the meal with a/an _____ cup of
                                   ADJECTIVE

  _____ rich cappuccino. The caffeine should give him a
       ADVERB

  buzz that will last all _____ long!
                               NOUN

FROM ADULT MAD LIBS™: HE LOVES ME, HE LOVES ME NOT. Copyright © 2008 by Price Stern Sloan,
a division of Penguin Group (USA), 345 Hudson Street, New York, NY 10014.

MAD LIBS® is fun to play with friends, but you can also play it by yourself! To begin with, DO NOT look at the story on the page below. Fill in the blanks on this page with the words called for. Then, using the words you have selected, fill in the blank spaces in the story.

Now you've created your own hilarious MAD LIBS® game!

STABBED BY CUPID'S ARROW

ADJECTIVE _____

VERB ENDING IN "ING" _____

PART OF THE BODY _____

EXCLAMATION _____

NOUN _____

NOUN _____

TYPE OF LIQUID _____

ADJECTIVE _____

ADJECTIVE _____

PART OF THE BODY (PLURAL) _____

ADJECTIVE _____

ADVERB _____

NOUN _____

PART OF THE BODY _____

PLURAL NOUN _____

PART OF THE BODY (PLURAL) _____

ADJECTIVE _____

MAD LIBS™

STABBED BY CUPID'S ARROW

It's February 14, and a/an _____ young woman is on her
ADJECTIVE

way to work. As she's _____ down the street, she
VERB ENDING IN "ING"

feels a sharp prick in her _____. "_____!" she
PART OF THE BODY EXCLAMATION

cries. "What was that?" Little does she know she's just been stabbed

by Cupid's _____! She looks around but doesn't see
NOUN

anything, so she heads to the _____ to get her morning
NOUN

_____. The _____ barista is the same one she
TYPE OF LIQUID ADJECTIVE

sees every day, but for some reason, today she finds him incredibly

_____. She bats her _____ at him. "Can I
ADJECTIVE PART OF THE BODY (PLURAL)

have a/an _____ coffee, please?" she asks _____.
ADJECTIVE ADVERB

When he hands her the _____, her _____
NOUN PART OF THE BODY

brushes against his, and she feels _____ in her stomach.
PLURAL NOUN

She locks _____ with him. "Thank you so much," she
PART OF THE BODY (PLURAL)

says. "Now will you be my _____ valentine?"
ADJECTIVE

FROM ADULT MAD LIBS™: HE LOVES ME, HE LOVES ME NOT. Copyright © 2008 by Price Stern Sloan,
a division of Penguin Group (USA), 345 Hudson Street, New York, NY 10014.

MAD LIBS® is fun to play with friends, but you can also play it by yourself! To begin with, DO NOT look at the story on the page below. Fill in the blanks on this page with the words called for. Then, using the words you have selected, fill in the blank spaces in the story.

Now you've created your own hilarious MAD LIBS® game!

YOU DON'T BRING ME FLOWERS

NOUN _____

ADJECTIVE _____

VERB _____

PLURAL NOUN _____

NOUN _____

ADVERB _____

NUMBER _____

NOUN _____

ADJECTIVE _____

ADVERB _____

ADJECTIVE _____

NOUN _____

PLURAL NOUN _____

NOUN _____

ADJECTIVE _____

ADJECTIVE _____

Today is your favorite _____ of the year—Valentine's Day!
NOUN

You wake up in a/an _____ mood and _____
ADJECTIVE   VERB

happily to work. Maybe your sweetheart sent a vase of fresh-cut

_____ to your office! Instead, you find a different surprise
PLURAL NOUN

on your desk—a/an _____ from your boss. It reads: "Report
NOUN

to my office as _____ as possible." The news is bad.
ADVERB

The company's stock has just dropped by _____ points
NUMBER

and the company is in danger of going out of _____.
NOUN

You can't wait for this _____ day to end. When you
ADJECTIVE

finally get home, you're _____ surprised to find your
ADVERB

_____ guy waiting for you. He gives you a tiny
ADJECTIVE

_____. You open it and find a pair of gorgeous diamond
NOUN

_____. You throw your arms around your _____
PLURAL NOUN   NOUN

in a/an _____ embrace. Maybe this wasn't such a/an
ADJECTIVE

_____ Valentine's Day after all!
ADJECTIVE

FROM ADULT MAD LIBS™: HE LOVES ME, HE LOVES ME NOT. Copyright © 2008 by Price Stern Sloan,
a division of Penguin Group (USA), 345 Hudson Street, New York, NY 10014.

MAD LIBS® is fun to play with friends, but you can also play it by yourself! To begin with, DO NOT look at the story on the page below. Fill in the blanks on this page with the words called for. Then, using the words you have selected, fill in the blank spaces in the story.

Now you've created your own hilarious MAD LIBS® game!

I.M. ME IF YOU LOVE ME

ADJECTIVE _____

SILLY WORD _____

NOUN _____

ADJECTIVE _____

ADJECTIVE _____

NOUN _____

EXCLAMATION _____

NUMBER _____

A PLACE _____

NOUN _____

ADJECTIVE _____

NOUN _____

NOUN _____

MAD LIBS™
Adult

I.M. ME IF YOU LOVE ME

An instant message conversation between two _____
                                                    ADJECTIVE

lovebirds:

QT3.14: hi, _____! how is your _____ so
                    SILLY WORD   NOUN

far?

Dreamy1: it's gr8, but I miss your _____ face. ☹
                                            ADJECTIVE

QT3.14: well, u will c me 2nite 4 our _____ date!
                                                ADJECTIVE

Dreamy1: u know it! i have a huge _____ for u.
                                            NOUN

QT3.14: _____! u r the best. i love surprises!
              EXCLAMATION

Dreamy1: i'll pick u up at _____ o'clock in front of
                                    NUMBER

(the) _____. make sure 2 wear your favorite
        A PLACE

_____.
    NOUN

QT3.14: sounds _____! when i c u, i'm going to give
                        ADJECTIVE

you a big _____.
                NOUN

Dreamy1: not if I can first, you naughty _____!
                                                    NOUN

FROM ADULT MAD LIBS™: HE LOVES ME, HE LOVES ME NOT. Copyright © 2008 by Price Stern Sloan,
a division of Penguin Group (USA), 345 Hudson Street, New York, NY 10014.

MAD LIBS® is fun to play with friends, but you can also play it by yourself! To begin with, DO NOT look at the story on the page below. Fill in the blanks on this page with the words called for. Then, using the words you have selected, fill in the blank spaces in the story.

Now you've created your own hilarious MAD LIBS® game!

THE HISTORY OF ST. VALENTINE'S DAY

ADJECTIVE _____

PLURAL NOUN _____

NOUN _____

NUMBER _____

PLURAL NOUN _____

ADJECTIVE _____

ADJECTIVE _____

PLURAL NOUN _____

NOUN _____

ADJECTIVE _____

NOUN _____

ADJECTIVE _____

PLURAL NOUN _____

PLURAL NOUN _____

ADJECTIVE _____

Many _____ legends tell the story of the martyred Saint
      ADJECTIVE

Valentine. According to one of these _____, Valentine
      PLURAL NOUN

was a Roman _____ during the year _____
      NOUN   NUMBER

AD when the emperor, Claudius II, outlawed marriage for young

_____. He believed _____ men made the
      PLURAL NOUN   ADJECTIVE

best soldiers. But Valentine continued to marry _____
      ADJECTIVE

couples in secret. When the emperor found out, he had Valentine

seized and put behind _____ where, it was said,
      PLURAL NOUN

he fell in love with a young _____ who came to
      NOUN

visit him. Before his _____ death on February 14, he
      ADJECTIVE

wrote her a/an _____, which he signed "from your
      NOUN

_____ Valentine." Today, lovers and _____
      ADJECTIVE   PLURAL NOUN

exchange _____ of affection on that date to
      PLURAL NOUN

commemorate the _____ Saint Valentine.
      ADJECTIVE

FROM ADULT MAD LIBS™: HE LOVES ME, HE LOVES ME NOT. Copyright © 2008 by Price Stern Sloan,
a division of Penguin Group (USA), 345 Hudson Street, New York, NY 10014.

MAD LIBS® is fun to play with friends, but you can also play it by yourself! To begin with, DO NOT look at the story on the page below. Fill in the blanks on this page with the words called for. Then, using the words you have selected, fill in the blank spaces in the story.

Now you've created your own hilarious MAD LIBS® game!

A LOVE SONNET

PART OF THE BODY (PLURAL) _____

ADJECTIVE _____

ADVERB _____

NOUN _____

ADJECTIVE _____

ADJECTIVE _____

PLURAL NOUN _____

ADJECTIVE _____

NOUN _____

VERB ENDING IN "ING" _____

ADJECTIVE _____

ADJECTIVE _____

NOUN _____

A PLACE _____

Adult MAD LIBS™

A LOVE SONNET

Love poems make you weak in the _____, so you're
PART OF THE BODY (PLURAL)

thrilled when your boyfriend sends you a/an _____
ADJECTIVE

sonnet. You _____ tear open the envelope and begin to
ADVERB

read:

Shall I compare thee to a Summer's _____?
NOUN

Thou art more _____ and more _____:
ADJECTIVE   ADJECTIVE

Rough _____ do shake the _____ buds
PLURAL NOUN   ADJECTIVE

of May,

And Summer's _____ hath all too short a date ...
NOUN

Suddenly, you stop _____. You've heard this
VERB ENDING IN "ING"

_____ poem before, but you can't quite remember
ADJECTIVE

where. Then all at once it comes to you. Your _____
ADJECTIVE

boyfriend has been plagiarizing the most famous _____
NOUN

of all time—William Shakespeare, the Bard of Stratford-upon-(the)

_____.
A PLACE

FROM ADULT MAD LIBS™: HE LOVES ME, HE LOVES ME NOT. Copyright © 2008 by Price Stern Sloan, a division of Penguin Group (USA), 345 Hudson Street, New York, NY 10014.

MAD LIBS® is fun to play with friends, but you can also play it by yourself! To begin with, DO NOT look at the story on the page below. Fill in the blanks on this page with the words called for. Then, using the words you have selected, fill in the blank spaces in the story.

Now you've created your own hilarious MAD LIBS® game!

THE BAD BOY

NOUN _____

PART OF THE BODY _____

ADJECTIVE _____

ADJECTIVE _____

ADVERB _____

NOUN _____

ADJECTIVE _____

NOUN _____

NOUN _____

NOUN _____

ADJECTIVE _____

ADJECTIVE _____

ADVERB _____

PART OF THE BODY _____

ADJECTIVE _____

You know this type of _____ well. He wears leather

NOUN

from head to _____, he rides a/an _____

PART OF THE BODY   ADJECTIVE

motorcycle, his wallet is always _____, and he's

ADJECTIVE

_____ self-involved. You know he isn't the right

ADVERB

_____ for you, but you just can't help the

NOUN

_____ way you feel about him. What's a good

ADJECTIVE

_____ to do? He may not be _____

NOUN   NOUN

material, but what the _____, you might as well have

NOUN

a/an _____ time while it lasts. Just remember to keep

ADJECTIVE

things casual and _____. If you find yourself getting too

ADJECTIVE

attached, end it _____. And whatever you do, don't give

ADVERB

him the opportunity to break your _____! That, after all,

PART OF THE BODY

is a bad boy's _____ specialty!

ADJECTIVE

FROM ADULT MAD LIBS™: HE LOVES ME, HE LOVES ME NOT. Copyright © 2008 by Price Stern Sloan,
a division of Penguin Group (USA), 345 Hudson Street, New York, NY 10014.

MAD LIBS® is fun to play with friends, but you can also play it by yourself! To begin with, DO NOT look at the story on the page below. Fill in the blanks on this page with the words called for. Then, using the words you have selected, fill in the blank spaces in the story.

Now you've created your own hilarious MAD LIBS® game!

MR. PERFECT

ADJECTIVE _____

ADJECTIVE _____

ADJECTIVE _____

ADJECTIVE _____

PART OF THE BODY (PLURAL) _____

ADJECTIVE _____

ADJECTIVE _____

ADJECTIVE _____

PLURAL NOUN _____

NOUN _____

NOUN _____

ADVERB _____

NOUN _____

ADJECTIVE _____

ADVERB _____

NOUN _____

Adult MAD LIBS™
MR. PERFECT

This Valentine's Day, you can't believe your _____ luck.

ADJECTIVE

You are dating the most _____ man. He's tall, dark, and

ADJECTIVE

_____. He has thick _____ hair, shining

ADJECTIVE ADJECTIVE

blue _____ , and _____ shoulders—and

PART OF THE BODY (PLURAL) ADJECTIVE

he is surprisingly bright and _____. On your first

ADJECTIVE

_____ date, he showed up right on time with a dozen

ADJECTIVE

_____. When he invited you over for an intimate

PLURAL NOUN

_____, you discovered that he even knows how to

NOUN

cook a five-star _____! And here's the best news of all:

NOUN

He's _____ neat and his apartment is always as clean

ADVERB

as a/an _____. Who knew men like him existed? Your

NOUN

friends call him "Mr. _____," but you know they're all just

ADJECTIVE

_____ jealous. You can't help it if the most wonderful

ADVERB

_____ on the planet chose you!

NOUN

FROM ADULT MAD LIBS™: HE LOVES ME, HE LOVES ME NOT. Copyright © 2008 by Price Stern Sloan,
a division of Penguin Group (USA), 345 Hudson Street, New York, NY 10014.

MAD LIBS® is fun to play with friends, but you can also play it by yourself! To begin with, DO NOT look at the story on the page below. Fill in the blanks on this page with the words called for. Then, using the words you have selected, fill in the blank spaces in the story.

Now you've created your own hilarious MAD LIBS® game!

DOUBLE BOOKED!

ADJECTIVE _____

NOUN _____

ADJECTIVE _____

PERSON IN ROOM (MALE) _____

ADJECTIVE _____

PERSON IN ROOM (MALE) _____

ADVERB _____

ADJECTIVE _____

PLURAL NOUN _____

PART OF THE BODY _____

NOUN _____

ADJECTIVE _____

ADJECTIVE _____

ADJECTIVE _____

NOUN _____

ADJECTIVE _____

Adult MAD LIBS™

DOUBLE BOOKED!

I'm a/an _____ single woman who's not about to be
ADJECTIVE

tied down by dating one _____. So when I found
NOUN

myself juggling two _____ men, I made Valentine's
ADJECTIVE

Day plans with both. I had a plan. First, I would have dinner with

_____. Then I'd make up a/an _____
PERSON IN ROOM (MALE)   ADJECTIVE

excuse about needing to be home early, and I'd have coffee with

bachelor number two, _____. Everything was going
PERSON IN ROOM (MALE)

_____ until number one insisted on walking me to my
ADVERB

door. Waiting for me was number two, holding a/an _____
ADJECTIVE

bear and a box of _____. His _____
PLURAL NOUN   PART OF THE BODY

dropped open. "These were for you, but now I'll keep them for

myself," he said as he stormed out the _____. I felt
NOUN

_____. But luckily, bachelor number one found the
ADJECTIVE

_____ situation funny and highly _____, so
ADJECTIVE   ADJECTIVE

I invited him in for a cup of _____. It turned out to be a
NOUN

pretty _____ Valentine's Day after all!
ADJECTIVE

FROM ADULT MAD LIBS™: HE LOVES ME, HE LOVES ME NOT. Copyright © 2008 by Price Stern Sloan,
a division of Penguin Group (USA), 345 Hudson Street, New York, NY 10014.

MAD LIBS® is fun to play with friends, but you can also play it by yourself! To begin with, DO NOT look at the story on the page below. Fill in the blanks on this page with the words called for. Then, using the words you have selected, fill in the blank spaces in the story.

Now you've created your own hilarious MAD LIBS® game!

THE LEGEND OF CUPID

NOUN _____

PLURAL NOUN _____

ADJECTIVE _____

PLURAL NOUN _____

NOUN _____

ADJECTIVE _____

PART OF THE BODY _____

A PLACE _____

NOUN _____

ADJECTIVE _____

A PLACE _____

ADJECTIVE _____

VERB (PAST TENSE) _____

PLURAL NOUN _____

ADJECTIVE _____

PART OF THE BODY _____

We all know Cupid as the winged _____ who shoots
                                              NOUN

arrows of love at _____. But do you know the legend of
                        PLURAL NOUN

this _____ god? Cupid was the son of Venus, the goddess
         ADJECTIVE

of _____. Cupid married a beautiful _____
      PLURAL NOUN   NOUN

named Psyche, but since she was a/an _____ mortal,
                                              ADJECTIVE

she was forbidden to look at him. But she couldn't resist a glance

at his _____. As punishment, Cupid dumped her and
          PART OF THE BODY

sent her away to (the) _____. Psyche wandered the
                            A PLACE

_____ searching for him. Her travels led to her
        NOUN

_____ mother-in-law, Venus. Venus had always been
      ADJECTIVE

jealous of Psyche, so she banished her to (the) _____,
                                                      A PLACE

where she fell into a/an _____ sleep. When Cupid found
                              ADJECTIVE

her, she _____. He realized he had deep _____
            VERB (PAST TENSE)   PLURAL NOUN

for her and they got back together. The gods rewarded Psyche

by making her a/an _____ goddess, free to look
                          ADJECTIVE

at her husband's _____ whenever she liked.
                      PART OF THE BODY

FROM ADULT MAD LIBS™: HE LOVES ME, HE LOVES ME NOT. Copyright © 2008 by Price Stern Sloan,
a division of Penguin Group (USA), 345 Hudson Street, New York, NY 10014.

MAD LIBS® is fun to play with friends, but you can also play it by yourself! To begin with, DO NOT look at the story on the page below. Fill in the blanks on this page with the words called for. Then, using the words you have selected, fill in the blank spaces in the story.

Now you've created your own hilarious MAD LIBS® game!

A LOVE LETTER

PERSON IN ROOM (FEMALE) _____

ADJECTIVE _____

PART OF THE BODY _____

ADVERB _____

ADJECTIVE _____

ADJECTIVE _____

NOUN _____

PLURAL NOUN _____

PART OF THE BODY _____

NOUN _____

ADJECTIVE _____

VERB ENDING IN "ING" _____

PLURAL NOUN _____

ADJECTIVE _____

ADVERB _____

PERSON IN ROOM (MALE) _____

Dear _____:
    PERSON IN ROOM (FEMALE)

I must confess my _____ feelings. Every time I see
                          ADJECTIVE

you, my _____ starts to beat _____,
         PART OF THE BODY   ADVERB

and I feel incredibly _____. Then you look at me with
                              ADJECTIVE

those _____ eyes and my _____ goes blank.
           ADJECTIVE   NOUN

_____ run up and down my _____, and I get
    PLURAL NOUN   PART OF THE BODY

_____-tied. You make me feel like a/an _____
    NOUN   ADJECTIVE

teenager. I am _____ this letter to let you know my
                VERB ENDING IN "ING"

true _____ because I don't know what else to do. I await
        PLURAL NOUN

your response with _____ breath.
                          ADJECTIVE

_____ yours,
    ADVERB

_____
PERSON IN ROOM (MALE)

FROM ADULT MAD LIBS™: HE LOVES ME, HE LOVES ME NOT. Copyright © 2008 by Price Stern Sloan,
a division of Penguin Group (USA), 345 Hudson Street, New York, NY 10014.

MAD LIBS® is fun to play with friends, but you can also play it by yourself! To begin with, DO NOT look at the story on the page below. Fill in the blanks on this page with the words called for. Then, using the words you have selected, fill in the blank spaces in the story.

Now you've created your own hilarious MAD LIBS® game!

BREAKFAST IN BED

NOUN _____

ADJECTIVE _____

PLURAL NOUN _____

PART OF THE BODY _____

PART OF THE BODY _____

PLURAL NOUN _____

PLURAL NOUN _____

NOUN _____

NOUN _____

ADJECTIVE _____

VERB ENDING IN "ING" _____

PART OF THE BODY _____

ADJECTIVE _____

NOUN _____

ADJECTIVE _____

Adult MAD LIBS™

BREAKFAST IN BED

Every man loves to be surprised with breakfast in _____.
NOUN

Here's a romantic recipe for _____ pancakes that
ADJECTIVE

will appeal to your guy's taste _____ and make his
PLURAL NOUN

_____ water. First, pour the batter into a mold
PART OF THE BODY

that is in the shape of a/an _____. Add chocolate
PART OF THE BODY

_____ and garnish with ripe, red _____.
PLURAL NOUN   PLURAL NOUN

Serve with a generous helping of maple _____.
NOUN

Put everything on a tray and present it to him with a copy of the

morning _____ and a/an _____ rose. After
NOUN   ADJECTIVE

he's done _____, give him a/an _____
VERB ENDING IN "ING"   PART OF THE BODY

massage. It's a/an _____ way to start the day. And
ADJECTIVE

who knows? He just may decide that he doesn't want to get out

of his _____ after all. In fact, he may have a/an
NOUN

_____ surprise for you as well!
ADJECTIVE

FROM ADULT MAD LIBS™: HE LOVES ME, HE LOVES ME NOT. Copyright © 2008 by Price Stern Sloan, a division of Penguin Group (USA), 345 Hudson Street, New York, NY 10014.

MAD LIBS® is fun to play with friends, but you can also play it by yourself! To begin with, DO NOT look at the story on the page below. Fill in the blanks on this page with the words called for. Then, using the words you have selected, fill in the blank spaces in the story.

Now you've created your own hilarious MAD LIBS® game!

LOVE COUPONS

ADJECTIVE _____

ADJECTIVE _____

ADJECTIVE _____

PART OF THE BODY _____

NOUN _____

ADJECTIVE _____

ADJECTIVE _____

NOUN _____

NOUN _____

ADJECTIVE _____

CELEBRITY (MALE) _____

ADJECTIVE _____

ADJECTIVE _____

Adult MAD LIBS™

LOVE COUPONS

Valentine's Day is about being thoughtful and _____. To
                                              ADJECTIVE
stretch out the goodwill, I present you with these _____
                                                    ADJECTIVE
love coupons. These coupons are good for . . .

• •

. . . a/an _____ back rub and _____ massage.
          ADJECTIVE   PART OF THE BODY

• •

. . . one delicious, home-cooked _____ and a/an
                                 NOUN
_____ dessert.
ADJECTIVE

• •

. . . a/an _____ breakfast in _____.
          ADJECTIVE   NOUN

• •

. . . a movie date—you pick the _____! And yes, even a/an
                                NOUN
_____ action flick starring _____ is okay.
ADJECTIVE   CELEBRITY (MALE)

• •

And to show my _____ love for you, these
               ADJECTIVE
_____ offers never expire!
ADJECTIVE

FROM ADULT MAD LIBS™: HE LOVES ME, HE LOVES ME NOT. Copyright © 2008 by Price Stern Sloan,
a division of Penguin Group (USA), 345 Hudson Street, New York, NY 10014.

This book is published by

PSS!
PRICE STERN SLOAN

**Look for these other fun Adult Mad Libs™ titles
wherever books are sold!**

Adult Mad Libs™: Advice for the Lovelorn

Adult Mad Libs™: Keepers and Losers

Adult Mad Libs™: Test Your Relationship I.Q.

Adult Mad Libs™: Party Girl

Adult Mad Libs™: Bachelorette Bash

Adult Mad Libs™: Dysfunctional Family Therapy

Adult Mad Libs™: Mama's Got a Brand-New (Diaper) Bag

Adult Mad Libs™: Who Moved My Cubicle?

Adult Mad Libs™: Kiss Me, I'm Single

Adult Mad Libs™: Retail Therapy

Adult Mad Libs™: Are You a Trick or a Treat?

Adult Mad Libs™: Santa Baby